Tests of Being

TESTS OF BEING

NUR CHEYENNE

KROSHKA BOOKS
Commack, New York

Creative Design: Gavin Aghamore
Editorial Production: Susan Boriotti
Assistant Vice President/Art Director: Maria Ester Hawrys
Office Manager: Annette Hellinger
Graphics: Frank Grucci
Manuscript Coordinator: Phyllis Gaynor
Book Production: Joanne Bennette, Michelle Keller, Ludmila Kwartiroff, Christine Mathosian, Joanne Metal, Tammy Sauter and Tatiana Shohov
Circulation: Iyatunde Abdullah, Sharon Britton, and Cathy DeGregory

Library of Congress Cataloging-in-Publication Data
available upon request

ISBN 1-56072-329-7

Copyright © 1997 by Nur Cheyenne
Kroshka Books. A division of
Nova Science Publishers, Inc.
6080 Jericho Turnpike, Suite 207
Commack, New York 11725
Tele. 516-499-3103   Fax 516-499-3146
E Mail Novascience@earthlink.net

All rights reserved. No part of this book may be reproduced, stored in a retrieval system or transmitted in any form or by any means: electronic, electrostatic, magnetic, tape, mechanical, photocopying, recording or otherwise without permission from the publishers.

The authors and publisher haven taken care in preparation of this book, but make no expressed or implied warranty of any kind and assume no responsibility for any errors or omissions. No liability is assumed for incidental or consequential damages in connection with or arising out of information contained in this book.

This publication is designed to provide accurate and authoritative information with regard to the subject matter covered herein. It is sold with the clear understanding that the publisher is not engaged in rendering legal or any other professional services. If legal or any other expert assistance is required, the services of a competent person should be sought. FROM A DECLARATION OF PARTICIPANTS JOINTLY ADOPTED BY A COMMITTEE OF THE AMERICAN BAR ASSOCIATION AND A COMMITTEE OF PUBLISHERS.

Printed in the United States of America

My poetry is written from a very deep, internal place–my gut.... My ability to get in touch with the depths inside me and to communicate these feelings is a gift from God and I am grateful for this.

Because one of the most important things for me in writing is honesty, it may be difficult to read some of this work. It is personal, some of it is painful...and about real life relationships.

— *NUR, IN A LETTER TO FRIENDS*

You have shown so many how to live with dignity and grace in the face of despair and death. You have risen again and again from heartbreak with the courage to endure more heartbreak. You had the courage and audacity to say yes to a life that has said no to you again and again.

Nur, you have fought the good fight and have won. You have won for all of us. For any of us who needed to see that it isn't what we win or lose but how we win or lose, you have set the standard...

— *IN A LETTER TO NUR, FROM HER BROTHER, BILL*

The most beautiful and profound emotion we can experience is the sensation of the mystical. It is the sower of all true science. He to whom this emotion is a stranger, who can no longer wonder and stand in rapt awe, is as good as dead. To know that what is impenetrable to us really exists, manifesting itself as the highest wisdom and the most radiant beauty which our dull faculties can comprehend only in their primitive forms, this knowledge, this feeling, is at the center of true religiousness.

Albert Einstein
What I Believe, 1930

There is a cyclone fence between ourselves and the slaughter and behind it we hover in a calm, protected world like netted fish, exactly like netted fish. It is either the beginning or the end of the world, and the choice is ourselves or nothing.

Carolyn Forche
From "Ourselves or Nothing," in
The Country Between Us

CONTENTS

Foreword	xiii
Preface	xv
CHAPTER I. THE CANCER INVESTIGATION	1
Tests of Being	3
Your Roving Eyes	7
Making Peace With Chemotherapy	8
Pushed	10
My Sweet Hair	12
Anger Transformed	14
Glad To Be Home	20
Absent Healer	21
Hope Is Fearing Hope	23
Absence	25
Now I'm Back	27
Fear Surrounds	28
CHAPTER II. BEING MOTHER	31
Born!	33
Being Mother: Ill	37
First Day	39
Oldest Son	40
War	43
Power Struggle	44
My Love For You, My Son	45

Your Pain	46
The Prom	47
The Cradle Rocks	48
My Second Son	51
Memories	54
CHAPTER III. STRAINED CONNECTIONS	**59**
Former Colleague	61
Deception!	63
The Gift	64
Changed	66
Princess	67
Words Not Touching	68
As One	72
CHAPTER IV. QUERIES OF THE SPIRIT	**75**
Volcano on Stage	77
Old Friend	83
Brokenness	84
Liquid Earth	86
Alone Time	87
Fear and Light	89
Lethargy and Lists	91
The Mirror	93
Banquet	94
The Search	95
Beast and Angel	97
The Fight	99
A Cocoon	100
The Meaning of Life	101
Pondskin	102
A Sacred Meditation	103
CHAPTER V. IN THE FACE OF DEATH	**107**
Want Ads From A Dying Woman	109

Slow Death	110
Without My Consent	112
Rain	114
All The Things I'll Miss	115
Anger	118
Not Yet	120
Overwhelming Loss	122
The Future of Our Moments	125
Nur's Prayer	126

FOREWORD

About three in the morning on March 10, 1991, Nur's father was awakened as he slept in a chair beside his daughter's bed. The room was quiet, but something had changed. Nur's breathing was slowing. Her face seemed to be fading. Bob quickly awoke other family members who hastened to gather around her bed. Then, as if she were waiting for them to send her off on a new adventure, she let go a small and peaceful sigh, and was gone.

I first met Nur in 1989 when my wife and I joined a wellness group of cancer patients, each of us afflicted with a different kind of cancer. With Nur and the others we traveled in this lifeboat for an hour and a half a week, pulling each other on board from the dark ocean into which we all occasionally slipped.

Nur suffered greatly with a difficult cancer, but somehow she found extraordinary courage without denying her darkest fears or running from her deepest losses. She lived more fully and longer than anyone ever expected.

She had a thousand things she wanted to do and, in spite of a dark underlining which was always much too critical of her limitations, Nur continued to work at her job in the New York State Department of Health, to be a single mother to two sons, to write poems, and take her chemo.*

For one of those years she wheelchaired to two of my creative writing classes and changed the lives of my students simply by being present. We all grew accustomed to her routines of survival and looked on in mute awe as she would inject herself with pain medication while talking from her heart, fully engaged in another's moment of fear or frustration.

---

*Part of this first appeared in *Voices, The Journal of the American Academy of Psychotherapists*, Vol. 27, No. 4 Winter 1991.

During her last year there were times when she began to feel herself pulling away from the mainstream of life, resenting that she could no longer participate. Though her parents were devoted to keeping her mobile, she began to envy the things well people take for granted like walking to the mailbox, chewing large overflowing sandwiches, and going to the movies. But always, through the full disclosure and animation of whatever was rising through her spirit, Nur returned to a center which seemed a bit calmer for each journey out, a bit brighter for each trip into darkness.

Truly, her eyes seemed to shine brighter as her body diminished. The more she struggled to stay alive, the more she bathed us all with this intense and Universal light. Soon, her battered, tired body seemed a buoy, marking where she was diving into waters humans still alive can rarely go, and then she'd surface, saturated with this light.

And now she is within us. She made sure of this, moment after moment, month after month, warming us each time she flared, and the heat of her spirit is under our skin. If she taught us anything, it is that though we part, we are never disconnected.

These painfully honest poems are what remain of a deep and brave spirit's journey back to God. They are a gift. And years from now someone we don't know or a godchild grown will ask about the spirit of the woman that would not die, and we will look at each other and try to say things no language can embrace.

One of the last things Nur said to me in a letter was, "The beauty of souls laid bare is that we are then all naked at once, together, our sameness and our differences revealed in the glory of the truth of us."

Nur's gift is that she laid herself bare and all who have the courage to look will find something of themselves in her.

MARK NEPO

PREFACE

Nur Cheyenne wrote most of these poems during the last three years of her battle with cancer. A divorced single mother, her work reflects the joys and sorrows, the courage and fears of raising two sons in a context of mounting losses and certain death.

This volume includes the poems that were in the manuscript at the time of Nur's death- plus thirty two others found in her writing notebooks after her death. A number of these were written during the last six months of her life.

Nur's original manuscript expressed appreciation for the advice and encouragement of Professor Mark Nepo and his Creative Writing class at the State University of New York at Albany.

Nur often expressed her gratitude for the love and support of a host of friends, coworkers, counselors, the staff and members of the First United Methodist Church of East Greenbush; also to the physicians, chaplains, and other caregivers at Albany Medical Center for their skill, openness, caring, and patience.

This collection was compiled by her father with the help of her mother, JoAnn, and her siblings, Bill, Ravi Har Kaur Khalsa, and Sharon.

ROBERT W. GORDON, EDITOR

Chapter I

The Cancer Investigation

TESTS OF BEING

My smile pasted on,
Humor forced,
My hand offered, a bribe
Persistently ignored.
I do not want to be here.
Do not want to have my body
Examined, poked, pushed,
My lungs x-rayed,
Bones scanned and
Heart
Raped
While you so clinically determine if those
    malignant cells lie quiet
Or run rampant through my flesh.

I am polite, even cooperative.
I swallow my revulsion
Of the tiny cubicle where I disrobe,
Donning hospital cotton soft and used.
Cloth bought cheap covers naked bodies all alike.
No longer uniquely myself,
I stand in line with others similarly condemned.
I fight the fear rising through my chest.
Once acknowledged, it would surely loosen the
    scream in my throat
And send me crashing through the halls with terror.

I sit quietly on the hard stool and wait.

The technicians are always young,
Their professionally memorized litany purposely
    void of emotion.
Knowing nothing of disease and pain
    and shattered hopes,
They crisply command me to "hop up here"
And "hold your breath."

I hate them.
Humiliated by my need for them,
They expose my failure to be healthy
And dare to compare their wholeness
    with my wounded self.

I try to remain calm, to imagine myself
    surrounded by Light,
But hearing voices requesting more pictures
My heart races, my throat closes, stomach rises,
Shutting off hope now trapped in my lungs.

Condescending and sweet, the voices
    remain impersonal
Though they view my very inner sanctum.
Without revealing its secrets
They tell me to get dressed.

"But what does it mean?"
I want to scream!
"Tell me, please,
Will I live this year?"

Are there more dark spots on these strong legs?
Is this bruise not really a bruise,
This sore, a sign?
Does my own flesh betray me?
I can't stand one more serious talk
    with my two sons,
Their world, again, torn apart
As they struggle in this living nightmare.

I'd rather not face more choices with no solutions,
More treatments with guaranteed side effects
    and unlikely cures.

But perhaps there is nothing there, sweet young thing.
Are these lungs clear, these bones strong
For one more six-month reprieve?
Can I move ahead just a few squares on this
Board of Life
Thinking positive thoughts,
Praying on scarred knees
That six months might become twelve,
That one year might become two...

The technician is silent as she
    removes the film.
She does not hear my screams.
No. Protocol says I must wait.
Only my sacred doctor with the MD after his name
Will divulge the results of this covert operation,
While countless others,
Not knowing my face,
My voice,
My soul,

Will analyze my blood
Read my bones
Stack their conclusions
In manila folders on a desk
Never understanding that
It is *me*
They discuss
And dissect,
It is *me*!

I embrace myself in a cocoon of rainbow hope,
A net of heartfelt prayers.
As I wait to hear
I arm myself with anger, strength, joy ...
I will *not* give up
I will *not* decide that all is done
No matter what their secrets say.

I know within my heart,
In the silent beating places,
That regardless of their answers

I am here
And I will be
Here always.

For it is not my flesh
That holds this heart
Nor my bones that cradle
This soul of softest silk.

I am here.

YOUR ROVING EYES

Your eyes graze mine briefly
Then move on...
The light of recognition
Does not grace your smile
And I remain
Shrouded before you
Hidden by a new face surgically prepared
With my permission.

But if I go to you...
If I turn and say
"Gloria, it's me, Nur..."
Your breath will catch in your throat
And the pain in your eyes
Will batter my heart
And cause me to mourn the future loss
Of faces I once owned.

Your questions are no different from my own...
Am I myself in this new skin
Or am I gone forever,
Changed by pain and loss
And mirrors that do not reflect
Familiar sights?

In the end,
The memory of your love
Is the bridge that reaches out to me,
Coaxes me to leap across
The chasm of your roving eyes
And walk into your life again.

Making Peace with Chemotherapy

An Invocation

You are chemical liquid, and cold...
As the mountain stream is running clear,
As the spring rain cascades through my arms,
As the winter snow is white and pure.

You are poison to parts of my body...
As the leaf of the lush rhubarb,
As the life-sap of the pine,
The red berry on God's bush.

I invite you in.
I open to you.
I request your presence here in this temple
That you might seek out what is misdirected;
That you might halt what multiplies unwanted;
That you might cease what grows without ceasing.

Under the golden heat of the sun,
Within the deepest blue of the sky,
Surrounded by the quiet beings of these giant trees,
Come work in me.

Come flow to those cells out of control
    and quiet their frantic race.
Come sweep calm through my veins
That life might seek its place within,
Content in measured grace.

I invite you to heal my being
From the inside out.
I welcome the signals you give
That this sweet nectar is reclaiming me.
So enter, dark liquid,
Bring your gifts to me.
And I will open
As God opens to me,
Asking only that you kneel quietly,

For herein, I am.

PUSHED

Frustrated! Mad! Annoyed!
Pissed
Pissed off. Pissed out. Shit down!
Pushing
Pushing myself to death
    Being pushed to death
        Falling into the cancer trap

Why can't I relax?
Pushing Pushing Pushing
    to eat
        to sleep
            to work
                to play
                    to parent

Pain
Pain pushes me
I push pain

Where is the time
Pushing for time
Time to learn
Time to resolve
Time to reconcile
    to know
        to love
            to be
                to be me
                    to be at peace
                    with me
                        and you

But time feels tight
And I feel pushed
So I push
And am pushed
And I don't know how to let go
Let be
Let down
Let in
Let off
Let to
Let you
Let me
Heal.

My Sweet Hair

They say two doses and I'll be bald,
Completely and utterly bald.
And it's not only my head
That will feel this breeze!
Open, naked to the air,
To your eyes, to my hands.
I'm scared!

Where will I hide?
What is left to save me from my mirror?
The truth of my asymmetrical face will be so bare
My wig lies will not suffice.

From days when "Buster Browns"
Were the "look" I sought
I've worried, fussed, cajoled and fought
To make these hairs go right or left,
Tuck here, curl there,
And wave in one direction only.

Now, it is only presence I seek
It's very being brings me joy.
Lingering before my glass,
I see each glint of light,
Each sweet reflection.

Tritely so, my life goes on
And one more new adventure is thrust my way.
Somehow, in some time, I'll learn
That I continue regardless
    Of mobility,
        Of mentality,
            Or emotion...

In fact, they say my hair will *grow away*
In death
When I no longer care.

Hard to end this poem about hair...
Hard to end hair...

ANGER TRANSFORMED

Like a wild wind rushing
    out of darkened skies
Anger flushes through my being,
Invading my mind with
    darkened blood.
Jaws clench in every muscle,
Eyes draw like slits
Closing out the light.
Anger takes over
    dictating staccato words,
Hardening my heart against
    forgiveness
As I rage against the men
    who took my life.

Yes. Because they were doctors,
    I believed them.
Because they were doctors,
    I trusted them.
Because they were white doctor
    men, I needed them.
And they questioned me,
They doubted me
They abused me and
Used me and
Cast me out when I did not
    fit their molds,
Would not get well at their command.

Left me shivering in the cold
With my pain
Clutching old tests that said nothing.

Requiring proper subservient behavior,
They accused me of madness
When tears poured from my heart,
Threatened if my inner screams
    were heard beyond my wall.

Questions were not allowed!
"If you do not believe,
You will not be healed."

When eight sweet hours of sleep
    eluded me for pain
I found myself undefended,
    sneaking around the halls
Like a truant looking for a smoke
    behind the gym.

You assholes!
You fucking self-righteous,
    terrified-to-be-wrong
Assholes!
There was a tumor there!
Eating up my face,
Creeping up my spine,
Invading my cells, my bones,
Creating unspeakable agony
Which, you announced,
I must learn to ignore,
Do my exercises and
Think positive thoughts, smiling through
    the shocking jolts up my cheek.

You corrupted me for your own use
And when I did not fill your bill
You dropped me like a sewer rat,
Laying the blame at my feet.
Calling me childlike, dependent
    and stung by divorce,
You tuned your face to those
    whose lives fit your story
And your incredible need to
    always be right.

And now this anger eats me up
As cancer eats my bones.
I feel the connection, yet feel
    helpless to unbind it.
I may be facing early death because
    my trust in you was broken.
How can I let go of anger
    whose origin may be my end?

Yet I do not want to die
    spitting and kicking
    at the world I love.
I do not want to fuel this
    bone-eating monster
With the rage that engulfs
    my heart,
Withholding forgiveness.
Withholding peace.

True. Anger has also been a
    good soldier,
A fighting companion that's kept
    me alive,
Slogging through swamps of terror,
Deserts of pain,
My anger at the thought of
    leaving my children
Building determination out of
    cement blocks.
My will to live has risen like a
    phoenix from the ashes of despair.
Disease licks her bones,
Yet still she walks, she talks,
    she lives, she lives.

I begin to look within, to peer
    beneath the anger.
To investigate the possibility
    of living without its shadow,
    of speaking without its voice.

At first I see no way.
Anger fills the corners and crevasses
    of my self.
Rage defines my response to
    memories I can't forget.
Forgiveness seems impossible,
Sits on tables like plastic flowers
    at the florists,
Dusty and unnamed.

I walk a little further in,
Breathe easier,
Feel quiet in my heart
As I ask for help.

"Ask Her," my friend says.
"Ask that part of you that knows,
That is Light, that is Whole.
Ask the Wisdom that is deep within."

I've done that before.
I've had contact with Her.
I've felt Her healing presence.
I've heard Her
Wisdom in my ears.

But I forget.
I forget She's there.
I forget She knows.
And each time I ask,
My voice is tentative with unbelief,
    trembling with fear
That she may not be there at all.

Slowly, I see her shimmer,
Not so clearly, just the Light.
Quietly I watch as she shows me
    who I am,
Prepares me for a ritual
    I've known before.

I don't understand.
It doesn't "make sense"
That performing this act
I knew as a girl
Will free me.

Yet I check my heart
Again and again.
The magic is unchanged.
She inducts me into mystery
And I emerge
Myself.
Unscathed.
No longer scarred by battles raging,
I walk softly, tall and proud.
I carry a staff carved with my symbol
And in this staff is my Power
Reborn.

Unknown to me, my anger
    gave it away to them
And it was not anger I needed to shed
But Power I needed to reclaim.

I feel, somehow, washed clean,
Released from a bondage that would
    not let me go.

How long must we languish in the
    prisons of our lives
Before we walk up to the doors
And unlock them with the keys
    before our eyes?

GLAD TO BE HOME

The warm, soft wind caresses my cheek
Bending palm fronds with a gentle push.
Light grey wisps float through that oceanic
    ceiling of blue
Briefly shielding us from the blinding rays of
January's lowering sun.

Shrieks of victory and occasional lament
Drift from the volleyball's court of play while
Neighbors grin at young tricyclers'
    adventurous peddling
And the music I abhor indoors accompanies
    my open stride
As I walk into this southwestern day in Arizona
Glad to be home.

ABSENT HEALER

Why must this healing hurt me?
Why must you insist that I be nothing
    while only you are something?
Why are my questions
    so resented, your answers so angry,
    my curiosity criticized?
Why do you refuse to see **me**
    as who I am?

What have I done to deserve
    such belittling?
If the pressure of what I ask,
    this healing,
Is too great, then refuse.

It is your yes, then no, then yes,
    that spins my head into crazy places
    and makes me doubt these vials
    you pump into my veins.

If it is healing you want,
    then heal yourself, dear one,
    of all this incredibly
    useless baggage
    you fling around the world.

Let your large ego step aside
    and allow the Spirit
    that comes with the wind
    to blow through your lab.
Let your mixing be led with
    your heart as well as
    your mind.

Release the pain you have
    collected and saved from your
    rejection by modern medicine.

If it is healing you want,
    learn that your very presence
    can bring healing or not,
That to bully a patient with knowledge
    is as damaging
    as pushing adriamycin
    into their veins.
You are surely led, your brilliance
    is a gift, but is it wise?

If it is healing you want,
    be willing to open your being,
    open your eyes
And stop scaring away every soul
    who just might,
    if you weren't careful,
    open your heart to love.

HOPE IS FEARING HOPE

Hope is rising in me,
A barometer of healing.
It reflects my body's new and able tricks.
To stand...
To walk...
To do the stairs as grownups do.
By god, this cane will go
While the wheelchair catches cobwebs
    in the corner!

Jauntily hope stretches out the door
    back to work.
My world expands beyond these walls.
Time dares to plan its future beyond
    next month.

Hope is rushing in on me!
Overcome with glee I'm grinning
    into chemotherapy
And bowing to the tree
That keeps my peace
And plays my God-connection role.
I'm thanking Universal truths
For unpredictable wellness,
And I'm welcoming life into my life again.

Hope is rushing in on me
Racing through my brain
Rousing my heart from soft cocoons
Into morning's wet new promise.

Yet, fear wakes too.
It hears the raucous laughing.
As Hope careens around a turn,
Fear looks sleepily over the edge at me
With solemn eyes.

Nervously, fear paces the lawn,
Hope's joyful antics giving pause
For always tailing Hope
Is disappointment.

Fear holds me back,
Skeptically polishing the cane in the closet.
Fear counsels an easier pace,
And flashes a wry smile on Hope's
    outlandish grin!

Fear will not sleep again now
Nor fully rouse, perhaps,
But will lie alert in the soft
    corners of my soul
Warily watching Hope enjoy her dance.

ABSENCE

Most times I no longer notice
Every moment
That he is not here,
That no love awaits me warming my bed,
No significant other embraces
    my yielding body
Stroking my longing arms and legs
Parting my lips with his,
Giving me his soul through
    liquid eyes.

No, my bed has been empty
Several years now, while
Illness seals its stamp
On my features
Robbing me of beauty
I once dared to claim.
Pain became too close a competitor,
The pursuit of health,
    of relief,
A rival too strong to challenge.

He left in despair, looking
    for joy, not agony,
Desiring to share pleasure, not pain.
And though I fault him not
(I could not love through this haze
    of narcotic cover-up)
I am enraged at this loss,
This hidden cost of illness,
This final blow!

Not only must I suffer this medical
    assault upon my being–
I must learn to endure it alone,
    without that special other to
    lean into when tides of
    weariness flood my soul.

Without another standing taller,
    straighter for my children,
    modeling wellness and stability,
Without that very special
    feeling of being loved and held
    and cared for no matter how my
    body feels.

Most days I can handle
    this absent lover.
I can feel incredible joy and
    incredible peace without him.

I manage my house, nurture my family.
It is not easy, but I can,

Until today
When, asked to perform a regular
    gynecological test,
You probed unmercifully
    into my nonexistent love life.
What did I use for birth control?
Do I have a boyfriend?
Am I sexually active?

    FUCK OFF!

Now I'm Back

So I walked on my own power
Back into these walls
Where I earn money
And craft my trade.
And people were glad
To have me back,
To see me upright,
Looking jaunty
Even in my wig.

But I felt tears
In my chest.
Sadness seemed to loll
Behind my eyes
All day and
Some dull pain
Throbbed deep within.
I could not name
The touched place.

Until on driving home
I realized the origins
Of those muffled sobs.
It's not that I'm back
Seeking dubious pursuits
Or that I had to leave
In pain and fear
Five months ago.
It's simply that I do not know
How long I'll be allowed to stay
And the joy of celebration
Has no half-life.

FEAR SURROUNDS

Today, when my eyes hit the sun,
Fear of the unknown
Washes over me.

Fear of life to come
Before death
Fear of death
Fear of losing
Of loss
Of losing more
Fear of being alone
Alone
The one to go
Alone.

I called Her,
The white, winged one.
I called Her to me.
To Light-flood me
To embrace me
To un-alone me.
I could not feel Her though
Or barely,
I could not find Her.
In my fear
She was not present.

Now, sunlight dapples through these pine trees
Birds call and drum their rap on wood.
Wind whispers through the tops
As all the crawling, flying, creeping bugs
    descend around me.
Beauty here.
Life here.

Can I suck it up?
Can I feel it in
My bones?
Can this earth-blessed sunlight
Bugsound air heal me?

CHAPTER II

BEING MOTHER

BORN!

Tightening!
Tightening!
Letting go
Letting out
Breathing easy
Tightening!
Tightening!
Letting go
Letting out
Breathe again.

Yellow blanket in the cradle
Tie-dyed t-shirt in the case.

Tightening! Tightening
Skin across belly
Pulls itself beyond its stretch.
Underneath, this being-babe
Gathers force of life
Ready for expulsion
Into oxygen!
Ready!
Ready!

Yet
Holding back.
Wants to stay in
Liquid home,
Always floating
Close to the drum.
The beating drum
Echoes in his ears.

Yet
Tightening skin
Pushes him new places.
Choice is gone.
Pressure builds.
Mother sweats, muscles arch
Pressing him downward.

My legs are quivering.
Light is low.
Efficiently he keeps track
One minute long,
Three minutes apart.

Eyes meet, locked in love,
Locked in wonder.
Who is coming?
Who will meet us at the door
    of this world?

Panting like a dog,
They said,
"Soon, soon."

Downward pressure
Pushes pounds through my body.
Vise-like, muscles deformed,
Stomach redefined in a second
One shape to another.

Suddenly! A swollen mass
Loosed in passage.
I know he is there!
The doctor is away with
Some pretty mom who let them
Stick her in the spine
To avoid feeling masses
In awkward spaces.

Wheeling through the halls
To some more proper place,
My breath comes in
Ragged, jagged puffs.
"Don't push!" nurse cries,
"Don't push!"

My whole body arches
In one triumphant push
Flesh contorts
Into the smallest cell
Only to push outward
Exploding!
Expanding forever!
From one body into two!

Slippery, white and red,
Your head appears
Deftly turned.

The cord unwound from round
    your neck,
Your body slides beyond my body.
Save one small strand of
    pulsing blood
We have been separated
Forever.

Loneliness engulfs me.
Once another body part,
Now, on your own.

I do not recognize such
    small beings...
Flat stomachs hold no promise
As I wander in search of you.
Reunited in your eyes,
Disbelief surrounds me.
Out of the forests of
    ancient time
I have found you.
One journey ended.
Another just begun.

In my youthfulness
I am frightened.
How will I care for you
Blue-eyed Wonder Boy?
How will painful, red-eyed tears
    be dried and
Baby rocked to sleep on breasts
Made full with mother's milk?

I hear your cry
Distinct from all the others.
My ears know you
And I beg for your release
Lest you feel lost,
Forever separate from your source.

They hand me a squirming bundle.
Eyes melt into souls
You are finally
Home.
My heart envelopes
All small fingers, all small toes
And licks the quiet tears
    of your asking.

BEING MOTHER: ILL

One is breaking away,
Desperate for a freedom
Rooted in a security
He never had.

The other clings,
Grasping for the womb
He feels wrenched from...
Angrily, he batters it
With his free hand.

Inept, we three,
Full of fury, hope and love
Warily circle each other.
Searching for morsels,
We snarl at the first one
Who tries to feed himself.

Wounded, slipping on floors covered
    with blood,
Each blames the other for not cleaning up
    the mess.

My heart weeps at my lack of first aid,
But, would you soften at my touch
Or push me toward the wall with your
    angry gaze?
You think I do not hear your pain?
I am bruised with the pain of your pain.

Helpless, I hear your cries
More clearly than you think
But I, too, am caged.
Caught in the solitary confinement of
    single parenting,
Trapped in a body crushed by pain,
I wonder if I'm really here.

Howling in front of the home cave
That, too, is your question.
"Where is my mother?"

My fear is that I will not learn to answer
Before my voice is gone.

First Day

One more day, God,
You've given me one more day.
But this day,
The first school day
    of third grade,
    of high-school seniors,
Feels like a year
Sitting golden in my palm.

Liquid pool of love, this day
I offer to these boys;
Blond, rushed,
Hair-combed, singing boys of mine
Off to school
For one more year with Mom,
One more promise
That I might be here
At the end of their day.

Tired.
Cranky, eager-telling-tales
Of the first day
    of third grade,
    of high-school seniors.
Thank you God
For liquid gold
In the palm of my hand.

OLDEST SON

Like ripples
from a pebble
dropped in pools of anger
your guilt spills
quietly
over my guilt
stemming
from her guilt
years ago
fostered
in my grandfather's house.

I hear my thoughtless spears,
casually,
yet accurately aimed for
your soft wounds.
I hear your cries.
Astonished,
you wonder aloud
why I draw blood
from my firstborn.

And I watch
in anguish
as my tone
catches your pain
which throws it back
in my face
accurately accusing me of abuse.

I am afraid.
I want only to love
but some loves, I know,
hold stinging hooks on tongues,
surround me with the barbed wire mesh
of shoulds and don'ts
and if-only-you-would-haves,
till love is transformed into a
field of mines...
and yours.

I try to reach you softly,
you do not hear me.
I speak more loudly,
you take offense.
I send you praise,
you hear maternal prejudice.
I caution safety,
you are overburdened by Homerule.

My imperfections
glare in your eyes.
Red-rimmed, choking on my own wordsores,
I see my misdemeanors
through your mirrors
darkly
Yet I know behind that glass
love lies
waiting.

Also hidden, muffled by your fierce and
embryonic independence,
fearful of discovery,
I hear your ever-present cry
for the love I want to give.

I wish my heart could reach
behind your eyes
And fill you with such loving space
that I cannot speak
and remind you that my womb
is your home forever.

WAR

Enemy.
I am.
You are.
We circle our bodies
Constantly blaming each other
For the blood
We draw from
Ourselves.

Son.
You are.
Mother, begging love,
I am
Wanting only peace
From your self-fulfilling anger.
Wishing once, acknowledgment
For some job well done.

Silence only.
Then recrimination.
Enemies aren't grateful
Even for clean battlefields.

If only I could play the medic
Patching wounds in the tent
And remember that machine guns
Will not fire
Unless picked up.

POWER STRUGGLE

Your clothes are picked up
(I'd made the request)
Almost, that is, not quite.
A few piles remain
Defiantly glaring at me
    from the floor.
Although it is my request
    for adherence to the "letter"
    rather than the "spirit"
    that so infuriates you,
You, yourself, obey the "letter"
    of my requests, not the "spirit."
Please clean off the stairs, I asked.
You did.
The dirty sox, sports array on the floor
    in front of the stairs remain
Laughing in my face.

MY LOVE FOR YOU, MY SON

Like the sun's rays deflected sharply
    from the mirror,
My love beats down on you, my son,
And traps you in the heat of
    your own reflection.
Like thorny vines fruited
    with rich berries,
My love has become enmeshed with
    your labor
To be free.

Stung by my own inadequacy,
I push forward,
Moving earth enough for three houses.

I'm so frightened that when
The sun dies down,
And the thorns dry up
I won't be here to watch
My love softly surround you
With the pregnant mist of
    your own being.

YOUR PAIN

Your life, entrusted to me
As smallest embryonic spirit
    becoming you
Has somewhere left the realm of
    cultivated rows and fields
Grows wild, without control
Though pinched by drought
    and undernourished roots.
You thrive somehow on deprivation
    and deprivation thrives on you.

You do not notice how truly
    green you are
        beautiful and strong
            uniquely blessed.

You have eyes only for the flaws
    glaring in your face
While your shattered dreams have
    become the focus of your life.

No words can be spoken
No actions commenced
That do not feel like piercing
    arrows to you.
Love is inexpressible,
Your ears are closed.

Of course, this rebel's work
Is yours to do these years.
Antipathy is ours to bear
While you urgently push away
    toward life.

THE PROM
FOR JASON AND CHRIS
JUNE 9, 1989

Swirling now under low, low lights
Tightly holding, gently
Each hand, each waist.
I imagine you lost in the stars of your eyes
The rainbows of your mouths.

No other night, Prom Night...
Leaning toward this night forever,
You dread its end
Dragging your feet through dances that
    take your breath away.

How can this satiny, bluish doe
    be in your arms, my son?
Have you sprung full-blown before me
    into manhood?
Waisted in that brisk cummerbund,
Broading shoulders proudly bearing
    this young butterfly.

A cascade of curls,
Her smile, a thousand times more bright than
    our gold orb,
You wear your hearts on your roses
And we can but hush
Before the candle of your promise
And the blush
Of our own longings.

The Cradle Rocks

Accusations like pointed slivers of glass
Rain on our bodies.
Suddenly this maternal cradle,
This womb-child bond is racked with
    earthquakes,
    hurricanes,
    and riots.

There are courtroom trials every day.
Who is the judge?
Both mother and son end up in jail
    reaching through the bars,
    terrified the separation
    will be permanent.

And it will be.
It is meant to be.

He must go.
That's it, you know.
He is only trying to tell her
That he must go now.

At first she feels guilty and rejected.
Why does he want to be away so much?
Always spending the night with friends—
Does he like their mothers better?
Later he screams, "I need to go!"
And when she is numbed into cold pain
By his declaration that she hates him,
He begs her for a hug.

He is so afraid that in pushing her away
He will push her away.

Later he cries because his dog is sad.
"I don't know why it is," he says,
"But I just don't want to play with her
    anymore."
"But," sobbing now, "I love her so much."

In a moment of gifted clarity she is able
    to respond,
"I guess it's kind of like not wanting to be
    with your Mom too much,
But still loving her a very lot."

"It's just like that," he says.

"Oh God," she cries out from her gut when alone.
"Now I understand.
He's simply leaving.
That's all.
And he needs desperately, incredibly, terribly
For it to be OK,
For me to affirm his ability to stand alone."

He needs me still,
He needs so much from me!
It's not that he doesn't need me.

He needs me to hug him whenever
    he wants me to.
He needs me to see him separately
    with his own life.
He needs me not to be hurt when
    he says I hate him
Not to care so much when he's angry.
He needs me not to be scared or hurt
    when he doesn't need me.

Dear God, I see now.
He needs me to let him go
And I will, now that I know
    what the battle is about,
I will, because I want to be free too,
And I know we can both win.

MY SECOND SON

It was your presence,
Your shining newest self fresh from
    birth,
That newly opened me to love.

It was with your touch,
Your holding, trusting gaze returning
That my heart softened,
Breaking open
To hear around its edges,
The silent, gentle lullabies of God.

As you grew,
Strangers stopped and smiled,
Then moved on,
Blessed by small energies
They did not understand.
Friends marveled,
Touched by that well of openness
Blossoming in your chest.
I sighed to hold you,
To hear your latest poem-thoughts on life.

I taught you nothing.
You are my teacher
And I am honored
In your presence.

Yet still the body of a small boy is yours,
Long, slim-limbed, more agile than athletic,
Rhythm-filled, this song'n dance man
    fills our home
With lively eight-year-old notes.

Why, then, was I torn from you?
Why was it *your* mother who filled with pain
Past the brim of understanding?
Why did you have to witness
Tears streaking my cheeks,
Screams filling our rooms,
Panicked terrors washing the floors
With the blood of a damaged reality?

Why were you, soft, young calf,
Asked to rise in silence,
A lonely bowl of Cheerios
Your morning mother,
A feeble kiss,
Your latch key out the door?

Why were you wrenched away,
No, taken,
No, given,
When I could no longer
Ask the neighbor to buy the Cheerios
And the feeble kiss
Became an effort I could not face?

For more long months than I want to count,
We were apart.
Months of illness
Months of terror
Months of questions with no answers
Of answers with no tomorrows.

And still this love I know is you
Kept me going
Kept me not giving up for good
Kept me angry for an answer
That would bring me back to you.

Now you are here and I am here.
The pain is gone,
The kiss is strong again,
But answers are complicated, uncertain.
What was once forever
Is now for today.
I cannot make the promises you so
Desperately want to hear.

I listen for the heartsounds of your being,
    your very Self...
They are present, but faint,
Muffled perhaps by the walls of protection
You have constructed
To surround this vital organ,
And by your justifiable anger
At so much absence,
At such incredibly, unreliable mothering.

I feel weak when faced with what you face,
Helpless to repair your unseen wounds
Which you insist are not there.
I feel so fucking, sadly furious that you,
Small, special gift of God,
Have been drafted into this unwanted war.

MEMORIES

As I board this aircraft in spring's
  hot blaze,
It hurts so much to be torn between
  home and Home.
Still on the ground,
Still in touch with Phoenix sun,
I long to jump and run off
  the plane
To yell Stop! Stop!
Don't leave. I'm not going!
I've made a mistake.
I belong here.

Guru Bahadur's smile, her bright eyes;
Guru Darshan's words about my poetry,
  her heart moved;
Dash Mesh howling for Mattagi,
  grinning, then howling some more;
Hargobind glancing up out of the
  side of his eyes, mischievous grin;
Karing Kaur's quiet presence,
  her silent knowing—then her quick
  slightly off-color jokes as
Sat Kaur does her work—caring
  for incapacitated me.

Hari Jap Singh of the bouncing step,
  one-pointed, happy,
  yet a yearning man.
Hari Simran, there's no light!
Hari Simran, there's no key!
Hari Simran, there's no paper!
"Sat Nam, Nur, Sat Nam."

Nirmal, steady worker, ready laughter.
Devi Dayal Kaur, smallest Sikh,
    of her own mind. This one
    will not be led astray
    from herself. She is Home.

Guru Roop Kaur, pure white
    with that flashy grin
    and earthy knowing,
Settled Sikh, yet never labeled,
She teaches me commitment
    and crazy cats.

Mere Piare, brother, friend.
Always known.
It took you three weeks to give me
    the hug that was already there.
I feel it still.
Your outrageous giggle belongs to
    some Guru I don't know
And the love that pours out of
    your heart
Belongs to us all.

Sada Anand's flashy smile,
    her exasperated-with-life sigh
    and
Nanak Dev in shorts and turban
Stalking macho-gutka images
That mirror his inner softness.

These I will miss,
    I crave.
These I call home.

Sat Bachan Kaur, Sikh mom, mom-Sikh,
    woman friend from always.
Freda, now Jass Want Kaur,
    teaching me myself,
    telling me herself,
Always open, always learning,
"Giving it to God."

These are etchings on my soul.
Not still lives, but moving dreams
    that go on forever,
Turban-topped and sandal-shoed
A family I never knew–
`A new identity as "Nur Kaur."

Yet there are those
At that other Home,
Fresh-faced
Grinning, heart pieces, children mine.
How could I belong where they are not?
How could home be Home without them?

They have lost me these eight weeks while
I have found me.
Here, in barren desert places
I have found the
Inner Core beyond prickly
    cactus skin.
Myself lies juicy in the secret
    darkness of Saguaro giants.

Can I take this home?
Does Home fly?
Will the person hugging my children
    this night be me?

Give me strength Lord.
Bring me your grace
And dry these tears
With your sweet breath.

Tell me that my Soul
Can ride USAir,
That intangible newest seedlings
    in my being
Will survive high altitude transport
And that the newly grown, healed
    Being that I am
Will always be me
Even under the pines in
    New York state.

CHAPTER III

STRAINED CONNECTIONS

FORMER COLLEAGUE

You ask to be my friend,
Still.
You want to gossip,
Kvetch,
Reveal the latest status
Of your loved one's musical pursuits,
Compare our children,
Share your loot from the recent sale.

You think nothing has changed.
That my loved one has become yours
Is simply a slight social sidestep,
Nothing to impede
An ongoing office friendship!

You have so much I do not have!
I have what you do not want.
You think I don't compare this disease
To your new house and husband?
My children ask for him,
What shall I say?
That illness wasn't his cup of tea?
But he really did like them...
How do I explain my empty bed,
That echoes in their hearts
    an empty chair
        an empty car
            and no ski trip in December.

Don't mean to hide behind these sons.
I miss him too.
Reaching out on starlit nights,
I remember his wild enthusiasm
For the universe.
I hear the symphony
And wait to know
Composer, artist and instrument
From his lips.
Passing the restaurants full of
    romantic couples
I remember being one with him.

And all the while I shared with you
His wonder and his pain,
His love and his doubts,
Our coming together,
Our breaking apart.

You took my wordy offerings
And married him
In my ill absence.

And you want to be my friend.

My heart is still stretching
To feel the pain.
It cannot stretch wide enough
To let you in.

DECEPTION!

Discomfort fills the air
As I dodge your kisses.
Sweating through my palms
I leak my anger into the air.
Stay away!

Your need engulfs me
As I drown at the edge
Of your desire.

Stay away!
Let me live!

And I will slap the part of me
Crying out for you
Every night at dusk.

THE GIFT

Losing him deepened pain
    I knew already,
Yet keeping him was suicidal.
Loss was etched in this young
    marriage before its birth
Yet I dripped with the blood
    of its going
And my bearings slipped sideways
    groping for some handle,
    some new place to stand,
As his life form faded from my door.

Left alone, not yet (one child
    in my hand, another in my womb).
I searched for love in hallways,
    on highways,
In darkened rooms at parties
Trying not to talk about
Babies coming,
My rounded belly screaming
For someone's touch.

Then he came. An older man.
A teacher, not a lover.
Friend, not a priest,
Yet somehow, he knew
    the rituals and masses
That needed to be said.
I gathered all my courage to
Look for clarity and wisdom
    in his eyes

So I could ask him what would
    happen and
Who would rescue me from the
Lonely prison of broken vows
    and the
Frightened promises of new life.

Eyes and hands were all he had.
They gripped round my heart
And surrounded me with peace.
On his voice came love greater
Than all the angels I had ever seen
And he offered me himself
With no holds barred.

Love rushed over me in tidal warmth
While tears left me helplessly open
To nothing but his gift.

He followed me home on
    the full moon
And gave me torches to light
    my way
When my faith grew weak.

Changed

If somehow accidentally
You stood before me
And years of anger,
Loss and loneliness
    fell away
So that it was long ago
And my heart still nestled
In your palm.
My eyes rested on your shoulder,
Still you would not know me
For my face has truly changed.
Altered by the surgeon's skillful knife
I am not the lover
Whose breast you sucked
On warm exciting nights
Not the woman whose legs
Entwined with yours
Seeking heat, seeking you.
I am not known.
Disfigured by disease
Shame crawls mercilessly
    into my mouth
While I watch your lusting eyes
Following her hips down the street.

PRINCESS

My rage is untenable.
Prohibited by lords and ladies fine,
It defiantly parades behind the
    dungeon walls of my fortress,
Its repulsive scent masked by rich perfumes
And incense smoldering on a forgotten altar.

Unpopular, in fact, unauthorized,
Yet bottomless,
This rage guards the castle moat with
    fierce monsters
And arms everyone with long pikes
And spikes
And ancient, heavy swords clanking.

Each passing caravan,
No matter how friendly or benign
Is greeted with the dragon's threats
Of torture or death by slow roasting
And the drawbridge slams shut with a
    resounding crash!

So why, the princess in the tower asks,
Does no one come to visit
Or stop by for tea?

Words Not Touching

On the road to your house
I remember
How I used to feel.
Leaning toward a nestling
In some space with you,
Our words embraced themselves
While two hearts opened
To the pain of being real.
Eyes bright with the newest
    tales of parenthood,
Questions of meaning hanging in the air,
Career dilemmas posed,
And we were shyly asking
Gifts of gentle guidance.

Always knowing love was present,
Hugs were free.
You were my friend
And all my truths were pages in a book
I wrote for you.

Suddenly disease exploded
On our world.
For years pain racked my body
While you tried to rock my soul.
I shriveled while you blossomed
And we watched each other
Helplessly seesaw into
Needy and needed
Sickly and strong
Depressed and fulfilled.

Fingers hanging tight,
Our attempts to keep on touching
Bloodied our hands,
Tore at our hearts
Until in one desperate moment
You flung your anger in my face
And its sting is like
A curse I cannot shake.

Now there is a wall around my heart.
Our words pass each other
Never touching.

Secrets go unshared,
Tales untold,
Hugs fall stiff and frozen on my back.

When you leave the room
Secret tears well silently.
When you return,
I can't tell if you are really there.

Politely smiling, I sit
In friendly postures
Stiff with phoney attempts to
    look intimate
From a great distance.

I want to ask you
What you meant,
And where you went
And if you mean to come back
Ever at all?
I'm afraid to ask you
What I did,
Why you left me
And if you think you'll ever care again?

Shall I foster this pretense?
An endless discussion of nothing
Over tea?
Or shall I risk even this
By addressing the truths
That lie waiting
In this empty space between us?

I'm so afraid of old angers
Rousing to ambush our newly
Intentional wish to be close.
I worry that my defenses
Will rise to protect
Behavior of which I'm not proud
While forgiveness looms untouched
In rooms we have not walked.

Most of all I know
There is a quiet empty space
Where you used to be.
And I fear that space in you
In which I moved
Has been filled with other shapes more
    pleasing,
Sounds that do not provoke your ire.

On the road to your house
I remember
How I used to feel.

As One

Gathering as always,
Eyes meet eyes
Hugs hold warmth.
Years have passed
As we've been circling
Round together
Plumbing pain, revealing anger,
Sharing joys, testing triumphs.
Always the circle's been there,
Always the arms are strong.

But today I'm feeling different,
Set apart
I don't belong.
Today I'm sitting separate,
Out of synch with a club that's moving on.

It's not just the wheels that are my legs,
The pump I wear attached to my heart.
Not just the medicines I inject
Or the baldness of my head.

It's that you're looking toward your life
And I'm looking back.
You anticipate some growth to come.
I pray that there is time
For more growth to be.

The flesh on your arms is thick
And without thinking
You shower and shave
    jump in your car
    drive to the park
    where you walk
    paths of sun
    and sit resting, cross-legged
    under a huge oak.
I sit painfully on the shower chair
    twice a week
    and wait for my friend
    to move my wheels outdoors
    where I may never again
    sit cross-legged on this earth
    under her beloved trees.

It's my turn to talk.
You really want to know how I am.
I know you do.
But I have no voice.
I can say the words,
    "new treatment experiment"
    "working at home now"
    "helpful new therapist"

This is only chatter.
My heart is silent
With separation,
Not knowing if I can ever be with you again.
My soul knows
If I do not speak my separated heart,
I never *will* be with you again!

Tears trickle down my cheeks
As I try to speak about not speaking.
Sorry I am and sad.
I am drawing lines between us
I don't know how to erase.
You look so different.
I feel alien.
My body scares me in this skin.

Slowly your hearts respond to my cries.
As you honor these walls I've built
They fall, gently, in a heap.
Quietly, one by one,
Your words hold me in my pain.

Sunlight filters across my face.
All of our hearts are open,
Soft.
Spirit fills the room now.
Hands join, heads bow in silent grace.
This moment, we are one.

CHAPTER IV

QUERIES OF THE SPIRIT

Volcano on Stage

I.

Molten!
Liquid rock!
Fires so hot that Earth
Is eating up her core with
    energy
White and radiant.
Belching through the orifice
Power seeks release.
Anger rages deep.
Melts the granite
At the center.
Ore heating ore
Searches the opening for
    overflow.

Permission denied!
Eruption disallowed!
Lava's not pretty on the stage
Of acceptable behavior.
Put on your hat, dear one.
Force those red hot thoughts
Down, deep down into your body
Where they can hurt
Only you.

II.

What source, this rage
What beginnings, such choking
Clogging hatred in my head?

A marriage bed betrayed
Not once
But once again and once again.
Badly soiled beyond repair
The sheets flung in my face.

Lovers found
Lovers lost
Losing self, a price too great
    to pay
For sex,
For joy.
Yet loss carves initials in my
    heart
And scrapes her raw sores
Leaving bloody flesh too
    ragged for sutures.

These fiery coals fill my
    belly
And freeze my feeling parts
Blue in the hurting time.

III.

Dig deeper, you say? Look
    further?
These betrayals are but plays
Upon a stage already set.

Search the dressing rooms.
Talk to the set designer.
Grab the director!
Interview the author!

It might be interesting.
Origins of rage may lurk in
    props, backdrops,
The cells of despair, born in
    dialogue,
Perhaps mundane.

IV.

An empty stage
Begins this play
Save one small child
Out alone, spotlighted
    and tiny.
No props.
No microphone.
Vanishing down the aisle
Her father opens the lobby
    door.

She tries a wave–
This fragile, skinny blonde,
A desperate attempt at
    connection
That would anchor her in
    safety.

He disappears.
She drifts, aimless,
Yet the cavity of her heart
    grows large
And echoes ominously in her breast.

Unprotected, she is assaulted often
In the name of family.
Both mother and brother find her
    fair game.
She learns their estimations
    of her worth are low.

V.

You've seen Act I.
Where is the review?
Can we engineer a rewrite
Full of warmth
And safe assurances?

Can we outlaw absence,
Pain and silence
With the smoldering embers of
    childhood?

To whom do I offer the icy, burning
    entrails of my being?
How do I empty this pit
Without vomiting up myself,
A raging beast left gasping on the
    shore
For air unavailable
To this particular species?

VI.

The stage brightens
Curtains rise.
Suddenly, a seraphim appears
Tall, whiteness streaming from her
    form,
Seared palms outstretched,
Made for embers,
Red, hot coals
Coughed up
One by one.

I stand before her.
Hunched with retching,
Each one comes with effort
Producing ember after ember
From my internal fires.
Perhaps as they touch
    her hands
Transformation will occur
Burning brightly,
Ever brighter.

Then, a flash!
Consumed!
Released!
Let go!
Only her palms remain
Facing upward, filled with love.
Her gaze accepts my eyes
As she patiently receives

Each small fragment
Of this buried burning,
Heaving up the emptiness,
    the silence
    the terrifying
    loneliness
Of rage.

VII.

At last, after centuries of gagging
    on this fiery bile,
After decades of offerings to this
    Angel of Light,
My body stands open
Now new,
Clean and cool.

Perhaps then, while I stand waiting,
Eyes locked with the winged one
Her being will begin to grow
And her spirit seem to permeate
The space I'm in.

Suddenly the mirror shatters!
The space between us dissolves.
Astonished then
I realize
That all the love in her eyes
Is for me
And from me
That she is me
That she has released me
And healed me.
I am whole.

OLD FRIEND

Pulled to you.
The gravity from your core
Reaches out to me
And I lean toward you
From miles away.

Your eyes force mine
Into a dance
While my ears
Flutter wide for each word,
Each phrase
Uttered in my presence.

My soul rests in your sight
Yet, also, bowing low
It twirls and leaps,
Deep in joy!

I know you!
You are old
Not new to me.
You present yourself in changed
    costume,
Or somewhat different voice,
But your message
Has been clear for centuries
And my heart is Home
In the Heart of your Heart.

BROKENNESS

To live in the stark raving honesty
Of all brokenness
To keep walking this path of glass
Sharp and lacerating
To move every moment
In the unhealed past,
In the wounding present,
The dangerous hurting of
    the future time.

To keep reading the story
When all the words have fallen
    to the floor,
Lie unfinished there
Saying nothing.

To keep getting up each morning
Moving into each day
With the dried blood of yesterday
Caking my palms
Flaking on my cheeks.
To feel each moment
With battered certainty
The searing ancient pain
Of not being good enough
    not being mother enough
    not being strong enough
    not being well enough
    not being tough enough
    not being tough
    not being.

To know with doubtful wisdom
That forgiveness cannot be bought
Is not for sale
And if it were, it could not cover
    the wounds,
Redeem the searing pain of blood,
Bind the hearts of brokenness
That lie here,
That forgiveness is out of reach
And this passage through
This broken land
May go on forever.

And yet to stand
On cliffs facing the sea
And hear my voice clear and strong
In channels of wind
Saying, Yes
Begin.

LIQUID EARTH

    Constantly combing the air with her
fingers,
    She lays her wetness on the grass like
a filigree shawl.
    Pouring her patterns in the mouth of
the Mother,
    Dripping descends down the throat of
the earth
    Quenching ancient thirsts unknown.
    Almost silently, deafening moistness
covers the eyes of the garden
as night moves in.

ALONE TIME

Pond
quiet ripples, circles, pebble drops
weeds bending
deer droppings
does the pond exist when I am not here
cool on the cheek
squishy muddy paths

loneliness cries out for me
spaces all around me touching emptiness
fear of being, fear of not
I hear the tension in me, stretching skin,
skin-stretching tension of loneliness,
fear of
    isolation, being caught
    the only one
    the only one here
    the only one around
    the only one left
    the only one without
    the only one without someone else

what if in this alone time
    with myself only
    it feels unproductive,
    not worthwhile?
what if I am not the person I
    choose to be with?

the past remains before time
memories are encapsulated in my head
memories of things the same and
    things different
people the pictures in my brain

yesterday walks up to my eyes and
    asks to come in
I do not know how to respond
do I remember peace or war?
reality gets misconstrued in this
    warm air embrace

God lives at the pond
    in the orchard
    in the stars
    in the skies
God present in me
    where?
    need to locate
    hollow place?
connection
connectedness
open, opening.
I help myself along, limping at my side
I take me over to another for introductions
tiredness is seeping in around the edges
under the lids
    my eyes droop
    my breath slows
    the pen stops
    my head drops
    parks itself
    in the quiet of sleep
    I escape into my dreams

Fear and Light

Shafts of early light
Stir me sweaty in my bed
Lids flutter fearfully
Not wanting to recognize
I have wakened
To the next day
Which might be one of my last.

Fear floods in
Crowds the sun
Crowds my plans
Will not speak below a dull roar
Fear takes up space
That might be used for healing
Fear is out of control.

Yet I feel Her Presence strongly
Angelic Being, almost me,
Hush. She beckons
Me
To open to Her Light
To release this to her.
I feel the Light touch the doorway
Of each cell
I feel the fear resist flinging doorways wide
Letting go
Letting in
The Light.

Flooded with Light
Each cell becomes more strongly itself,
More uniquely its own
More clearly who it is
More faithful to the truth.

Its own being less apt to be tricked
By the trickster
Disorganized by the disorganizer
Less vulnerable to cancer patterns
Replaying on its screens.

Open
Open up
Each cell
Each doorway
Open to Light.

LETHARGY AND LISTS

My lists runneth over with the necessary
Without which surely my life would collapse.
My body is tense with the energy
Needed to procure, drop off, sign for,
    clean up, and prepare
For life
(In case it comes up on the list).
My mind races creating more
    lists within lists
Always keeping track of what has been done
But mostly of what has not.

Must goals and rituals, tasks and errands
Be my drug of choice
With well-accomplished self-esteem
    the high I seek?
Am I a doing junkie with souped-up adrenals
Looking for my hourly fix of chores?

I know when the last item is scratched
The last list completed,
Cupboards stocked, wash clean, toilet gleaming....
I know then I'll take time to relax.
Then I'll slow enough to really enjoy the
    kids.
When I've finally worked hard enough to prove
It's OK to make money
I know I'll find ways to let go for a few
    hours
Each week,
Or maybe even a few minutes
Each day.

Saddest of all,
This addiction to getting it done
Forces even the fun things on the list
And a moment of silent meditation
Becomes a line to be crossed off.

So perhaps today, a day of lethargy
    and uneventfulness,
A day when no letters got written,
Bills paid
Or errands run,
A day that unfolded unplanned
When the list never made it out of my pocket,
Perhaps this day was a beginning
Of more uneventful days,
Days that will never be noteworthy,
Days that will unfold from meal to meal
With no plan
And no structure,
End with no heroic epithet,
But simply slide into night with a
    meaningless sigh.

And yet, on one of these uneventful days,
Magically, mysteriously, I might realize
Beyond all reason
That the very deep core of my unique self
Is still OK.

THE MIRROR

My Higher Self gives me a box
With a mirror
Look and love, she says
Look and love.

She loves me.
Sometimes I feel it
Rolling over me in waves
Filling every inch of me.

She loves all of me.
Even ugly anger
Even black scary places
Even my screams, she loves
She loves all of me.

Sometimes I feel it
Feeding the hungry, hurting parts in me
Healing the rough, sharp edges of my fear.
Leaves me filled.
More full.
More open.
More loved.
More me.

BANQUET

when the center of
my very body becomes
a clear, pure stream
when the sun's rays
penetrate my heart
at some velocity
beyond the speed of light
and then the scent
of pine and burning leaves
and old lawn mower gasoline
smoothly fills my lungs
with breath
then the presence in my heart
expands beyond itself
while only Joy invites
me to this banquet
of her treasures.

The Search

No wonder I feel cut off, not having
 written for days,
Not connected with myself.

Yesterday I felt so alone
Lonely
The only person I know really
 facing this moment,
Separate and cut off from
 those around me
Who are so healthy
So *continuing* in their lives.

I fantasize about a "dying commune"
All who are terminal could go there
And experience together their last
 days and hours,
Learning from and through each other.

I *want* to open my heart to
 my experience.
I *want* to be able to let go of this
 life when it is time,
To trust God that what awaits me
 is more of what He/She is,
 trust that I am ready for that.
I *want* to be able to be loving
 and peaceful with those around me,
 not angry and bitter, full
 of jealousy and resentment.

Sometimes I am jealous of my own
    dear parents
For their opportunity to live so long
    together.
Then I feel guilty for taking so much
    of their time
Crowded by their space.

I want to pray.
I want to write eloquently
    like Frederick Buechner.
I want to be able to evoke
    in myself and others
The deep, spacious, everlasting
    power of God.
I want to be able to speak into
    and out of the Silence.

Why?
So I will hear.
So my heart will be opened.
So my voice will be heard
By me
As well as others.

BEAST AND ANGEL

Fear
crushes my chest, makes the air come hard,
It hurts to breathe.

Courage
takes a deep breath,
alert, relaxed...
Her heartbeat steady.

Fear
blinds, I cannot, will not see
what is there.

Courage
looks fear in the eye
staring it down.

Fear
the unknown, the unclear,
secret, dark, afraid of itself.

Courage
starts out as fear,
Cannot exist without it.
Drawing strength
from fear itself,
courage blossoms and unfolds.

Fear
throws the bolt and pushes the chair
under the knob.
The window is never open.

Courage
expands from darkness to light.
Walks openly, revealing itself, unembarrassed.
The door swings wide for friends.

Fear grows by itself, with no food, no water,
out of control, a malignant beast.
Fear is wild, unrestrained, unwanted growth.

Courage halts the growth of fear
boldly beckons it to enter, yet refuses to
introduce it to guests.
Courage feeds itself nourishment from nowhere.

Fear leaves me alone with itself.
Silent, afraid to scream,
afraid to look,
afraid of fear.

Companions, they trot side by side,
each hopes to surge ahead, to gain the race.
Two sides of the mirror, one looks in, one out.
My choice is who to feed
And how to recognize
Not the Beast, but the Angel.

THE FIGHT

The fight is fearsome, painful and long
Only those who win come out strong
It means battling terror
It means brooking no error
It means types of treatment
    bringing horror unimaginable.
Meditation
Visualization
Vitaminization
Nutrition support
Dark drops of seaweed
Send me energy, send me life.
Castor oil packs
Garlic juice drinks
Carrot cereal and crystal amulets
Have I done enough now?
Can I stop this frantic show?
I'm trying to prove to someone
That I'd like to live awhile
But is he listening?

A Cocoon

Wrapped in silky threads
Quietly I rest
Nestled in the hopes of tomorrow.
Softly, my beating heart
Betrays my lively self
Though movement cannot occur through
    metamorphosis.

Structure does not last,
Are these legs or wings?
Only in the windows of my soul
Do answers lie covered under the
    wheelchair's tracks or
At the tip of my pen's fine stroke.
This cocoon has no bars
    but the ones she has spun herself
And silky threads make fine trapeze strands
In this garden.

The Meaning of Life

Some days
Meaning hangs in the air
Dripping
With the fresh scent
Of reality.
Armored with this newness,
She dips
From time to time
    Into hope,
        Into fear,
            Into courage,
While everything is laced with
Love
Which surrounds the whole of meaning
Everywhere.

Some days
Meaning is not present.
Emptiness fills up her eyes.
Unprotected from this odor,
She dips
From time to time
    Into pain,
        Into loneliness,
           Into despair,
While everything is laced with
Love
Which surrounds the whole of meaning
Everywhere.

Pondskin

Somewhere in all this density
I feel there is
A still openness
A vast beginning
I call God
Intimately recreating itself
Out of Joy.
Yet fear erases feeling
Terror stills my listening
I cannot feel or hear this God
When I fear I won't.

Sometimes when your eyes meet mine
I feel a soft, small space
Begin to open in my chest
A current moves between us
Some vibrancy surrounds us
And a Presence moves in quietly
Connecting us to stars
No longer there.

A SACRED MEDITATION
A THANKSGIVING FOR JULIE PRESS

Written after attending a conference entitled
Awakening to the Sacred Presence Within Us

Being a guest,
I walk quietly
into all the
rooms you have prepared.

Full of unknowing
I tell my own story
of dragging the pain
shackled to fear.

Being a guest
you offer me cleansing.
Washing gently, I lift away
layers of scales covering my eyes.

Silently opening
the door before us offers
an entry into the Never-seen.

Gently rocking,
you suggest I awaken
from sleepless nights
into the moment of now.
Trusting you mostly,
grasping my flashlight
I peer into black velvet caves
that open to streams
which flow into oceans of skies
that cradle the stars
who radiate light forever.

Being a guest
my heart is expanding
my eyes are more seeing
my soul is more welcome
than when I force my way in.

Fear is still present
sitting beside me.
I ask it to wait before speaking
(it has nothing to say).

In this expansion
life is more present.
It opens before me a widening road.
Ever branching, many choices,
its riches surround me.
Jewels shimmer within me.
I am a gem.

Being a guest,
Death is an Innkeeper.
The no-vacancy sign
lies unused in the shed.

Watching the lights in the Inn,
they beckon to travelers
when they are ready.

Being a gem,
I build my own dwelling
across the field.
Walking my choices,
Living my Heart,
I garden my flowers
and water my plants.

Being a gem,
Abundance is flowing.
I'm sharing tomatoes
with the Innkeeper's cook.

Being a being
Always I'm grateful
for God within you,
within me, within them,
bringing me blessings,
lifting my eyes and
expanding my vision

till all of my breath
is all there is.

This poem first appeared in *Voices, The Journal of the American Academy of Psychotherapists*, Vol.27, No. 4 Winter 1991.

Chapter V

In the Face of Death

WANT ADS
FROM A DYING WOMAN

ONE SUMMER VACATION with a certain nine-year-old son. Beach and sun a must. Will take sand and crabs, rocks and spiders. Wishing for discovery, companionship, silliness and memories to build a life on–must be wheelchair accessible.

ONE BOOK OF POEMS, published under my name. Winning wide acclaim for startling honesty and sparkling language. Talk shows pick up immediately, fame blossoms as book sells widely.

HUSBAND, LOVER, FRIEND of many years. Soul mate in whom I would continue to live, to whom I could leave my children in total trust. Sexy, loving partner who gives me courage to fight, who is devastated by my possible absence, unafraid of life's challenges. If applying, must be willing to sign on retroactively–time is of the essence.

ONE LARGE MEASURE OF FORGIVENESS from my children, my friends, my family, for the demands, the time, the selfish views, the crabbiness of me and illness. And for all my failings as a person, my inability to be who you might have wished me to be at any given moment, please offer me forgiveness and love me anyway.

ONE MIRACLE CURE–out of the pile of possibilities, out of the depths of despair, regardless of the unfairness of life and death, sickness and health, I request one miracle cure, a reprieve from unwanted early death, a chance to live out who I am more fully, more completely, more appreciatively than I ever dreamed. The gift of life given back. Please apply immediately. Time may be short.

SLOW DEATH

Aching back
Stiffening legs
Still carry me
But the pace is slow.
Fear creeps
Into the creases
In my brow.
Am I speeding up or
Slowing down?

Can this slow death
Be stopped
Or has it just begun?

How can my body be so far behind
My heart
Springing with warm life
Soaring into soul truths longing for
    expression
Wondering at flowers in bloom?

Most days I feel too alive to be dying
But in these last few
Achy bending catches me short
And tells me
Maybe this is real,
This bodily destruction
Occurring within.

Caught between wanting to live Life
While Life is here
And needing to care
For a body that cries for rest,
I hang on a bridge of denial
That equates
Rest with death.

I am so afraid of losing life.

WITHOUT MY CONSENT

Death
Where are you?
Are you not as near
As last night's sleep?
Though I have long pushed you away
I feel you close.
I know you beckon
With Life's love in your heart.

You are getting acquainted with me
And I with you
But you will always know me better
For you are Unknown.
And though I trust the Light
And walk the path of God
Yet still you are in shadows,
Dark and still,
And I am frightened by the mirror
Which throws me no reflection,
Frightened by the deepening sound
That has no echo,
Frightened by the Universe
Which has no edge.

I will come to you
Finally, undoubtedly,
Because I have no choice.
I'd like to walk in open-eyed,
Not dragged, screaming across
    the threshold,

But the Light in me will have to
Bubble-up...
Will have to widen
And slowly overtake the shadows
That reach for my last breath.

The trick, I think, is
Learning to breathe
Light.

RAIN

Reminding me of long-held tears within,
This rain pours out of skies
    thick with grey.
Wetness opens all my wounds and
Sting's the skin's softly
    sensitive crevasses.
There are no partners in this rain dance.
It is a dance I dance alone
As sadness wells up from bottom places.
My pain leaks out of the corners,
    cracks and crooked window sills
    of my body
While I rush inside desperately
    sealing these betraying fissures.

ALL THE THINGS I'LL MISS

I thought I'd write
Of all the things I'd miss,
The things I'd never do or be
If I die a younger death.
Then maybe I could
Stop thinking of them,
Their hold on my brain might loosen
And my heart
Could open to who I've been
And who I am
And maybe even to who I might
Still be.

A happy, active fifty-year-old
Gardening with a fervor
Traveling with curiosity
Working always toward my Center,
Writing, more and more of me.
This I'll never be, perhaps.
This me, you'll never see.

A grandmother for these two boys
A grey-haired mom to help
And sit and
Keep my mouth shut
While I love the grown-up kids I've got
Indulging *their* children
A little overly much.
This, they might not have, my kids.

Will they tell of me?
What will they say?
Will they remember anything
Strong and good and clear?
Will they tell those little ones
How I would have loved them,
How I would have cared?

An older woman in love
Falling in my early sixties
For some wonderful companion
For life's endtimes
Thriving on joy and openness
Picking up old tricks
Like weaving and potting in spare time
Finally clear in my own profession
Of groups and therapy
Sharing the mysteries I love so well
The mysteries I choose
As the path of my heart.

This I won't feel or have.
No older lover for me this life
No winding down time
For gathering in the old loves
Or rekindling activities
From younger hands.
No time to savor the riches.
Instead, feeling robbed
Raped of wholeness
Battered away from completion
Finished too early
Not yet ripe
Unfull, unready.

Or I could look behind
At fullness
At gifts
I could give thanks
For many inner gifts found and used
With friends.

For children's births
Miracle times full of glory
For parents that take a prize,
And sibling love unrivaled
Revealed.

I could give thanks
For grace that touched my heart
With God
Many, many times each year
For friends whose hearts have
    traveled with me openly,
Who opened me.
For writing words that touched some tears
Began some smiles
Spoke to soft and bloody places.

I could look back
And see the riches,
The jewels
The incredible landscapes of my life
And thank God for what I've had.
I guess what makes that so hard is
Early landscapes
Speak of wonderful colors to come.

It is difficult to give up.

Anger

My anger knows no bounds
It reverberates through my being-body
Bouncing from tumor to tumor
Cell to cell
Wreaking havoc and horror
Playing damage
Creating hell.

I'm angry at my parents
That they read to prepare for my death
I'm angry at my friends
That they detach from my loss
Run from my fear
I'm so angry that they all get
    to go on living
That they are not me
That only I am me.
Only I, it seems, have to end
    what I do not want to end.

I am full of rage
Full of cancer
Perhaps they really are the same thing.
How can I ever empty myself of this anger?
I can feel that it blocks the love
That it shadows the Light
How can I ever channel it
Voice it enough to be through.

I resent even having to do it!
Yet I want to find the Light
Somehow I really want to find it
Or
I will live alone
And die alone
Whenever those activities begin.

I do not know how to hope for life
In the face of death
I do not know how to face Death
As I hope for Life!

NOT YET

Sadness overtakes me now
The sun shines unendingly
But only grey surrounds my heart
Snapping my throat shut with a bang!

No treatment last week
Blood counts too low
Cancer too strong
It eats through my bones
Erodes my Spirit.
Trust and hope
Take long walks in the woods.

I would run after them
But my legs can barely guide
    the wheelchair.
My weight can stand one moment
To let the dog out.
So hope and trust
Run free under the pines.
I don't know whether they'll return.

I am not ready to die,
Damn it!
There is still too much to do
And I want to do it!

I don't want to let go of my body
In the cold winter months.
Let me stay till spring wraps us warm.
Let new life be part of my death.
Let the pond waters be open and
    the ground receiving my ashes
Gentle and soft.

Then I will go.
Ready or not.
I will go–
If you pull me there.

Overwhelming Loss

Only my sadness fills me now.
My cup overflows with tears
And they are all for me.
My losses are too great to count
Too deep to measure accurately
Is there anything left, but loss?

It is not just losing my life
But so many smaller deaths along the way
Till I feel all amputated from myself
Cut off from who I know myself to be
And scared.
Losing courage also.
Losing.
Losing.

Lost two years of pleasure just to pain
Pain came and took it away
Hid me in a closet tight
While I struggled to breathe.
Pain chased away my lover
Frightened my children
Hurt my job
Pain took my love of God and Life
Crashed it in the trash
Like a mirror shattered.
Pain laughed at me
Called me a joke!
I even heard the angels laugh.
I thought I was alone.

Then cancer came
Took the pain away.
I was glad and brave.
Frightened, but strong.
OK, it had a name
Cancer.
Adenocystic carcinoma of the left
    parotid gland.

It took my face this time.
The I who was me disappeared
And someone else is here.

Sad. Sad. Sadness here.
Cancer wants to win.
Each time I do my best.
I look upon it with fearless eyes
To search for treatments far and wide
To endure the pain, humiliation and loss
Of movement, loss of hair, loss of job.
Yet still it stalks me
Will not give me up to Life
Will not let me stay in Peace
In Joy.

True. My transformation may not be
    complete.
Each time I returned to Life
Was I changed?
Where was the new me
Who understood that Life is Precious
Time is now
Children only for this moment?

Was I not too often caught up in
 unimportant things
Not flushing my anger
Not living my joy
Busy erranding my body to death?
Yet isn't that a part of life
That can't always be escaped?
And haven't, please God, oh haven't
I tried my best
To integrate it all?

I am sad, today.
Under these giant trees
That have not healed me
I am sad.
I call out to the Universe
To the stars at the edge of my sky
Help me. Help me live
Or
Help me die...
But, help me, please, help me.

THE FUTURE OF OUR MOMENTS

The future is not with me.
Unreal, as always,
It tempts me with its lacy patterns,
Golden sunsets
And grandchildren hidden from view.
Has time collapsed or expanded?
I cannot know.
Only that the past
Holds seeds of futures yet unfurled,
And that the crystal moment of now
Gives birth to the
Real future,
Shrouded with secrets,
Yet somehow truer to life
Than my imaginings.
We may not have the future of our dreams,
But the future of our moments is always with us.

Nur's Prayer

Dear Father/Mother God,

    Please help me live today in your fullness, in your ecstasy and in your faith.

    Surround me with your light that makes me well and whole, and walk with me through the valleys of fear, doubt, distrust and anxiety. Lend me your strength.

    Dear One and only Spirit, fill my spirit with your Light and your understanding. Direct my energies and activities toward Love and give me the time and energy I need to fulfill my promises to myself and others.

    Thank you for your care, for my very special care-givers, for all that I have been able to do and all I want to do. Thank you for my sons. Truly they come from you. Amen.

February 23, 1991

Nur died March 10, 1991.